Other giftbooks by Helen Exley:
A Megabyte of Computer Jokes   A Portfolio of Business Jokes
Cat Quips   Golf Quips

Published simultaneously in 1998 by Exley Publications LLC in the USA and Exley
Publications Ltd in Great Britain.

12 11 10 9 8 7 6 5 4 3 2 1

Copyright © Helen Exley 1998.
The moral right of the author has been asserted.
Edited and pictures selected by Helen Exley.

ISBN 1-86187-089-2

Exley Publications Ltd, 16 Chalk Hill, Watford, Herts WD1 4BN, UK.
Exley Publications LLC, 232 Madison Avenue, Suite 1206, NY 10016, USA.

A copy of the CIP data is available from the British Library on request. All rights
reserved. No part of this publication may be reproduced in any form.

Pictures researched by Image Select International.
Printed in China.

Acknowledgements: The publishers are grateful for permission to reproduce copyright
material. Whilst every reasonable effort has been made to trace copyright holders, the
publishers would be pleased to hear from any not here acknowledged. JOE CLARO:
from *The Random House Book of Jokes and Anecdotes*, edited by Joe Claro. Published by
Random House, Inc. STUART CRAINER: from *The Ultimate Book of Business Quotations*,
published by Capstone Publishing Ltd. © Stuart Crainer 1997. GUY KAWASAKI: from
The Computer Curmudgeon, published by Hayden Books, US. © 1992 Guy Kawasaki.
BERNARD LEVIN: from *A Walk Up Fifth Avenue*.
Picture credits: Exley Publications are grateful to the following organizations for
permission to reproduce their pictures: The Image Bank: cover and pages 6, 8, 12, 16, 20,
24, 28, 32, 40, 44, 54, 58; Pix: title page and page 50; Telegraph Colour Library: cover.

COMPUTER QUIPS!

NE521D
DA133
9109K

A HELEN EXLEY GIFTBOOK

EXLEY

"What sort of a day did you have at the office, dear?"

"Catastrophic! The computer broke down and we all had to think!"

EDWARD PHILLIPS

Each decade brings a 300-fold increase in the complexity available to the computer.

At this rate, computers will exceed the complexity of the human brain between about AD 2010 and 2020.

Sadly, whatever we do to advance our powers, we can also do for robots... and they are likely to be faster thinkers than we are.

Perhaps they will be kind enough to keep us as pets.

CLIVE SINCLAIR,
CHAIRMAN OF THE BRITISH BRANCH OF *MENSA*

TEN COMMANDMENTS
FOR COMPUTER OPERATORS

1. Always work as part of a team.
That way you always have someone else
to blame when things go wrong.

2. The best way to keep your job is to get
things so mixed up on your first day that they
can't afford to fire you.

3. Beware of any computer installation
that has heel indentations all up
and down the front of it.

4. Anything you learned about computing
systems two weeks ago is already
out of date.

5. Don't waste time trying to work out your mistakes. Work out who to blame.
6. Never let the computer know you're in a hurry.
7. Try to become involved in the decision-making process. Insist on their letting you toss the coin once in a while.
8. There's never time to do it perfectly, but there's always time to do it again.
9. Plugging it in might help.
10. If all else fails, read the Manual.

EDWARD PHILLIPS

The world was once divided into those who used computers and those who did not. No more. The new world is divided into those who have watched helplessly as their computers have crashed and those who are waiting for it to happen.

STUART CRAINER

THE COMPUTER IS DOWN;
IF OUR WORLD NEEDS AN EPITAPH, AND IT MAY,
COULD THERE BE A BETTER?

BERNARD LEVIN,
FROM "A WALK UP FIFTH AVENUE"

Over the new office computer
was a large sign which read:
TODAY IS THE TOMORROW
YOU WORRIED ABOUT
YESTERDAY.
A week later somebody
had added:
AND NOW YOU KNOW WHY!

MILTON BERLE

THE SIX PHASES
OF A NEW COMPUTER
INSTALLATION:

1. General enthusiasm.

2. Complete confusion.

3. General disillusionment.

4. Search for the guilty parties.

5. Punishment of the innocent.

6. Promotion of non-participants.

RICHARD S. ZERA

When does a computer
become obsolete?
The day after you learn
how to use it.

HILTON BERLE

YOU KNOW
YOUR COMPUTER
IS OBSOLETE WHEN
It starts every sentence with
"It wasn't like that in my day...."
It's more than two weeks old.
A new piece of software comes onto the market.
It's the year 2000.
The strange burning smell becomes overpowering.

STUART & LINDA MACFARLANE

DEFINITIONS

Compress: Reducing size of files you should throw away.

Computer conference: A collection of computer executives in a resort bragging to each other about how smart they are.

Diagnostic program: A program to tell you what you already know: your file is fried.

Electronic mail: A method for receiving messages you cannot understand, from people you don't know, concerning things you don't care about.

Hard disk: A device that enables you to keep files you don't need.

Multimedia: The unnecessary in search of the undoable.

Test drive kit: A demo version of software intended to convince people to buy something they don't need, from people they don't trust, with money they don't have.

Server: Software that enables other people to crash your computer.

Warranty: The time period during which your computer does not break.

GUY KAWASAKI,
FROM "THE COMPUTER CURMUDGEON"

Computer Expert: someone who can take something you already know and make it sound confusing.

The function of a computer expert is not necessarily to be right but to be wrong for more sophisticated reasons.

EDWARD PHILLIPS

IT Consultant: someone who saves his client almost enough to pay his fee.

FRED METCALF

WHY A COMPUTER IS BETTER THAN YOUR DATE

– *Computers can be switched off when you are finished with them.*

– *They never say "You can't log on tonight, I have a headache."*

– *They remember everything you want them to remember but forget everything you want them to forget.*

– *They are always willing to listen when you talk.*
– *They don't get annoyed when you forget their birthday.*
– *They are not rude to all your friends.*
– *They don't dump you for other people.*
– *They don't get jealous when you spend time with other computers.*

STUART & LINDA MACFARLANE

The world of work
is intimidating.
After years of college
and post-graduate
study
plus work training,
they sit you at a desk
in front of this tiny
little machine
that's cleverer
than you are.

ELIZABETH COTTON

THE INTIMIDATING COMPUTER

In the old days
it was important to be able to run down
an antelope and kill it
with a single blow to the forehead.
But that skill
is becoming less important every year.
Now all that matters
is if you can install your own Ethernet card
without having to call tech support
and confess your inadequacies
to a stranger whose best career option
is to work in tech support.

SCOTT ADAMS, CREATOR OF DILBERT

ADULTS LEFT IN THE DUST

"Arithmetic is easy for you,"
said the five-year-old to his father.
"You can work it out in your head.
I have to use a computer!"

MILTON BERLE

The Ministry of Defence once sent an order
to Ladybird Books for a title
on the workings of computers.
When Ladybird Books pointed out
that their books were aimed at children
of about nine years of age,
the Ministry of Defence thanked them
for the information and confirmed the order.

DAVID HARDY, FROM "WHAT A MISTAKE!"

*Progress is when you replace
a £200 a week clerk with
a £2,000,000 computer.*

GILDA PETROV

Nowadays an underprivileged family
is one that is making do
with last year's word-processor.

Computer manufacturers
are planning to tell their customers
how long their computer systems
will last.
Two minutes longer
than the final payment.

EDWARD PHILLIPS

LAWS OF COMPUTING

By the time a program has been completely
debugged it is obsolete.

Programs will expand to take up all
available memory.

There is always one more bug.

Computers always crash the day before
you do a backup.

When finally you buy more memory
you will not have enough disk space.

The price of a computer will be slashed
the week after you purchase it.

All computers are obsolete.

Printers go faulty ten minutes prior
to an important meeting.

A computer makes more mistakes in two seconds
than twenty people working for twenty years.

Your password always expired yesterday.

STUART & LINDA MACFARLANE

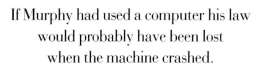

If Murphy had used a computer his law
would probably have been lost
when the machine crashed.

MIKE KNOWLES

A COMPUTER
CAN WORK OUT A COMPLICATED
MATHEMATICAL COMPUTATION IN A FEW MINUTES
— A JOB THAT WOULD TAKE A HUMAN MIND
MANY YEARS TO COMPLETE.
HOW DOES IT DO THIS?
IT MAKES EVERYTHING UP.
WHO'S GOING TO SPEND YEARS CHECKING IT?

DAVE BARRY

<u>YOU KNOW YOUR COMPUTER IS *FEMALE* IF</u>

- *The manual is 600 pages long but the first 590 are devoted to setting the screen colour and fonts.*
- *You have to wait 30 minutes for it to get ready before it will do anything.*
- *It expects you to buy it flowers.*
- *It wants to talk incessantly.*
- *There are more than 100 items in its CD drive.*

STUART MACFARLANE

YOU KNOW YOUR COMPUTER IS *MALE* IF

- *Within weeks of purchase you find a better model.*
- *It looks neat and tidy until you get it home.*
- *Every few minutes it emits a "burping" noise.*
- *It has a 12" monitor but believes it is 18".*
- *It refuses to do anything for your mother.*
- *It performs well in the lounge, mediocre in the bedroom and not at all in the kitchen.*

LINDA MACFARLANE

EAT YOUR WORDS...

I think there is a world market
for maybe five computers.

THOMAS WATSON, CHAIRMAN OF IBM

There is no reason anyone
would want a computer in their home.

KEN OLSON, PRESIDENT AND FOUNDER OF
DIGITAL EQUIPMENT CORPORATION 1977

Computers in the future
may weigh no more than 1.5 tons.

FROM "POPULAR MECHANICS"

http://w.

http://www.

http://www.

The more a speaker uses multimedia,
the less he or she has to say.

The more fonts in a document,
the less content it has.

Electronic mail...
turns average Joes and Janes into
swaggering John Wayne-
Steven Seagal-Chuck Norris-
Charles Bronson-mutant-ninja-
electronic assassins.

GUY KAWASAKI,
FROM "THE COMPUTER CURMUDGEON"

If you put tomfoolery into a computer, nothing comes out of it but tomfoolery. But this tomfoolery, having passed through a very expensive machine, is somehow ennobled and no-one dares criticize it.

PIERRE GALLOIS

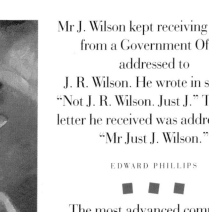

Mr J. Wilson kept receiving E-mail
from a Government Office
addressed to
J. R. Wilson. He wrote in saying,
"Not J. R. Wilson. Just J." The next
letter he received was addressed to
"Mr Just J. Wilson."

EDWARD PHILLIPS

The most advanced computer
in the world was asked:
"How did the world begin?"
It answered:
"Refer to Genesis, Chapter 1."

"READER'S DIGEST", 1972

A computer consultant was called in to repair a faulty machine. He studied it carefully and then struck it a resounding blow with a large hammer. The computer sprang to life at once.
His bill was thousands.
As he explained later, "The huge bill was not for hitting the machine with a hammer. It was for knowing where to hit!"

EDWARD PHILLIPS

Jargon: what computer programmers talk when they don't know what's going on.

REX MALIK

Analyst Programmer:
the incompetent writing
the incomprehensible.

REX MALIK

Software Processing Engineer:
someone who will know tomorrow
why the things he predicted yesterday
didn't happen today.

FRED METCALF

Computer experts:
"The longer the title, the less important
the job."

GEORGE MCGOVERN

YOU KNOW YOU HAVE BEEN SPENDING TOO MUCH TIME AT THE COMPUTER WHEN...

You do not pay any bills because
they have not been E-mailed to you.

When reading a book you look
for the scroll bar to move
to the next page.

You double click on light switches
to try to turn the light on.

You try to save the newspaper every
ten minutes just in case
the system crashes.

STUART & LINDA MACFARLANE

Using an artificial intelligence programme,
the first ever computer joke
has been generated.
It goes

"010011010101100111011"
Well computers think it's funny.

D.J. FLEMING

A brand new giant computer
which could answer any question put to it,
was asked,
"What will the world be like in fifty years time?"
Unfortunately,
they couldn't read the answer –
it was in Chinese.

"READER'S DIGEST", 1971

YOU KNOW YOUR DATE IS A COMPUTER ADDICT WHEN . . .

He wants to tell you all about the great database he has created to log all the trains he has spotted.

His car sticker says, "My other computer is a laptop."

He has IBM tattooed on his arm (unless his name is Ian Brian MacDonald.)

She has several disks in her handbag
but no lipstick.
He introduces himself as
simon@moron.twit.com.
She speaks six computer languages
but no foreign languages.
He invites you home to see his new
computer hardware and shows you
his new computer hardware.

STUART & LINDA MACFARLANE

Computers are fixtures in our offices,
in our homes and in our cars.
There is no escape. The only consolation
is that PCs don't yet eat and drink.

STUART CRAINER,
FROM "THE ULTIMATE BOOK OF BUSINESS
QUOTATIONS"

I've heard that myth
quite seriously expressed in my church,
that the Beast in the Book of Revelations
will be a monster computer.

BILL ELLIS,
FROM THE "INDEPENDENT",
13TH DECEMBER, 1994

" NOTHING CAN GO WRONG…"

The world's first fully computerized airliner
was ready for its maiden flight
without pilots or crew.
The plane taxied to the loading area automatically,
its doors opened automatically,
the steps came out automatically.
The passengers boarded the plane
and took their seats.
The steps retreated automatically,
the doors closed, and the airplane taxied
toward the runway.

"Good afternoon, ladies and gentlemen,"
a voice intoned.
"Welcome to the debut of the world's first
fully computerized airliner.
Everything on this aircraft is run electronically.
Just sit back and relax.
Nothing can go wrong...
nothing can go wrong...
nothing can go wrong...."

JOE CLARO,
FROM " THE RANDOM HOUSE BOOK OF JOKES"

I DON'T BELIEVE THE THEORY THAT MODERN LIFE
IS BECOMING IMPERSONAL AND COMPUTER-DOMINATED.
AND MY WIFE, 674 DOT 391 BACKSLASH 4088,
AGREES WITH ME.

ROBERT ORBEN

A computer addict's wife complained to her husband, "You never take me anywhere! You're always playing with your computer! You never even remember our anniversary. I bet you've even forgotten the date of our wedding!" "Of course I haven't," said the husband. "It was the day I bought my 266 MHz Intel Pentium II processor!"

ANDRE DE ROCHE

"My partner told me last week he'd leave me if I didn't stop spending so much time with my word processor."
"What a shame!"
"Yes – I shall miss him."

MARIA MASTRANTONIO

<u>WHAT</u> EXTRA EFFICIENCY!?

Computers make it easier to do a lot of things,
but most of the things they make it easier to do
don't need to be done.

ANDREW S. ROONEY

The main impact of the computer
has been the provision of unlimited jobs
for clerks.

PETER DRUCKER

Computers are a splendid invention.
Think of the time they've saved us
which we can use straightening out all the mistakes
in computer billing.

EDWARD PHILLIPS

Isn't it strange that computers today
can do things that twenty years ago
weren't even thought worth doing?

GENE PERRET

"Install 1"

No matter how much
you use your PC,
no matter how quick
your little fingers move,
"Install 1"
is the disk you will need
most often.

HAZEL MNISI

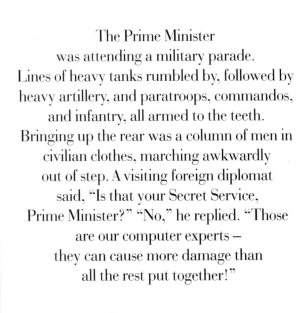

The Prime Minister
was attending a military parade.
Lines of heavy tanks rumbled by, followed by
heavy artillery, and paratroops, commandos,
and infantry, all armed to the teeth.
Bringing up the rear was a column of men in
civilian clothes, marching awkwardly
out of step. A visiting foreign diplomat
said, "Is that your Secret Service,
Prime Minister?" "No," he replied. "Those
are our computer experts —
they can cause more damage than
all the rest put together!"

GEORGE COOTE

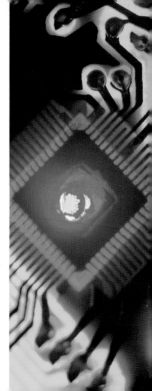

IF THE WORLD BLEW UP
TOMORROW,
THE LAST AUDIBLE
HUMAN VOICE
WOULD BE A
COMPUTER PROGRAMMER
SAYING
IT COULDN'T HAPPEN.

EDWARD PHILLIPS

By the light of the Moon

by Elizabeth Dale
illustrated by Jill Newton

Ladybird

It was eight o'clock and the zoo was quiet. All the visitors had left. The elephants snoozed, the hippos yawned and Charlie, the keeper, was saying goodnight.

"Goodnight, Charlie!" said Caz the chimp, giving Charlie a big sloppy kiss through the bars.

"Goodnight, Caz!" said Charlie. "And don't get up to any mischief!"

"Me? Mischief?" asked Caz, quietly unclipping Charlie's great big bunch of keys.

Here's a story to share!

Sharing a story with your child is great fun and it's an ideal way to start your child reading.

The left-hand pages are 'your' story pages. The right-hand pages are specially written for your child with simple vocabulary and helpful repetition.

• Cuddle up close and look through the book together. What's happening in the pictures?

• Read the whole story to your child, both your story pages and your child's. Tell your child what it says on his* story pages and point to the words as you say them.

• Now it's time to read the story again and see if your child would like to join in and read his story pages along with you. Don't worry about perfect reading – what matters at this stage is having fun.

• It's best to stop when your child wants to. You can pick up the book at any time and enjoy sharing the story all over again.

Here the child is referred to as 'he'. All Ladybird books are equally suitable for both boys and girls.

Edited by Lorraine Horsley and Caroline Rashleigh
Designed by Alison Guthrie, Lara Stapleton and Graeme Hole
A catalogue record for this book is available from the British Library

Published by Ladybird Books Ltd
27 Wrights Lane London W8 5TZ
A Penguin Company

2 4 6 8 10 9 7 5 3 1

© LADYBIRD BOOKS LTD MMI

LADYBIRD and the device of a Ladybird are trademarks of Ladybird Books Ltd

Goodnight, Caz!
Goodnight, Charlie!

5

Caz looked around the cage. Gordon was picking fleas off Loz. Tommy was swinging backwards and forwards with his tongue out. It was much too quiet.

Suddenly Caz jumped up.

"Wake up the tiger
and the kangaroo!
I've got the keys
to all the zoo.
Wake up the monkeys
and the big baboon!
Let's all dance
by the light of the moon."

Let's all dance by the light of the moon.

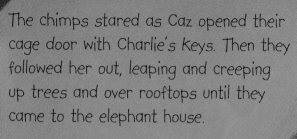

The chimps stared as Caz opened their cage door with Charlie's keys. Then they followed her out, leaping and creeping up trees and over rooftops until they came to the elephant house.

The elephants were just nodding off.

Suddenly Caz burst in and said, "Come out and play!"

Come out and play!

9

Caz climbed up Jumbo's trunk and
onto his back.

As the elephants rumpeted
and trumpeted along, Caz sang...

"Wake up the penguins
    and the rhino, too!
I've got the keys
    to all the zoo.
Wake up the crocs
    in the green lagoon!
Let's all dance
    by the light of the moon."

Let's all dance by the
light of the moon.

11

The lions and tigers were just settling down for the night. The leader of the lions yawned an enormous yawn. Tanya the tiger kissed her cubs goodnight.

Suddenly Caz burst in and said, "Come out and play!"

Come out and play!

The lions and tigers, cheetahs and leopards came roaring and pawing out of their cages.

"Let's go and wake up the bears!" said Caz. And she sang...

"Wake up the bison
    and the great big gnu!
I've got the keys
    to all the zoo.
Wake up the snakes
    and the striped raccoon!
Let's all dance
    by the light of the moon."

14

Let's all dance by the
light of the moon.

The bears were snoring as they dreamed of cool streams and tall trees. They looked as harmless and gentle as teddy bears!

Suddenly Caz burst in and said, "Come out and play!"

Come out and play!

The bears woke up straight away.
Then they rollicked and frolicked
right out of their cages.

"Now it's time to party," said Caz.
And she sang...

"Now that we're all
    wide awake,
We've got lots
    of noise to make!
Just strike up
    some groovy tunes,
And let's all dance
    by the light of the moon!"

Let's all dance by the
light of the moon!

The bear band started to play, with Barney on the bugle, Belinda on the big bass drum and Bertie on the banjo.

Everyone cheered and said, "Look at the bears!"

Look at the bears!

The elephants were the best dancers.
Jumbo span around on his trunk, and
Emma and Eddie waltzed in time to
the music.

Everyone clapped and said, "Look
at the elephants!"

Look at the elephants!

The animals danced and had so much fun
that they soon forgot about the time.
No one was tired any more.

Exhausted at last, Caz sat down and looked
at the sky. It was starting to get light.

Just then the clock on the keeper's house
started to strike. It was morning!

"Oh, no!" said Caz. "Look at the time!"

Look at the time!

The animals ran back to their cages
as fast as they could.

Leaping and creeping, trumpeting
and rumpeting, roaring and pawing,
rollicking and frolicking, they got back
to their cages just as Charlie
came through the gate.

And Charlie had no idea what they'd
been up to. Well, almost no idea...

Look at that!

Turn off the TV, close the door, too.
Here's a story to share for just me and you...

Inky-pinky blot

Who is the inky-pinky blot in the dark, dark pond? He asks everyone who goes by, but no one ever seems to know…

Caterpillars can't fly!

A baby caterpillar dreams of flying high in the sky but all her friends just laugh. What is she to do?

By the light of the Moon

Charlie the zoo keeper has gone home and the zoo is quiet. Now it's time for the animals to dance by the light of the moon…

Molly Maran and the Fox

It's cold outside and Molly the kind-hearted hen says all the animals can stay in her warm barn. But how will she keep out the wily fox?